Black Bears

Victoria Blakemore

For Sir, who is always there to listen or make me laugh.

You're no vegetable lasagna!

Table of Contents

What Are Black Bears?

Black bears are large mammals. They are the smallest kind of bear that is found in North America.

Most black bears have thick, black fur. Some black bears are more brown or tan in color.

Many black bears have a lighter

color of fur on their **muzzle**.

Size

Black bears can grow to be up to seven feet long. They stand up to three feet at their shoulders.

Adult black bears have been known to weigh up to 600 pounds.

Male black bears are usually

larger than female black bears.

Physical Characteristics

Black bears have very thick fur. This helps them to stay warm when it is cold outside.

They have rounded ears that stand up straight. This helps them to hear prey. They often hear other animals before they see them.

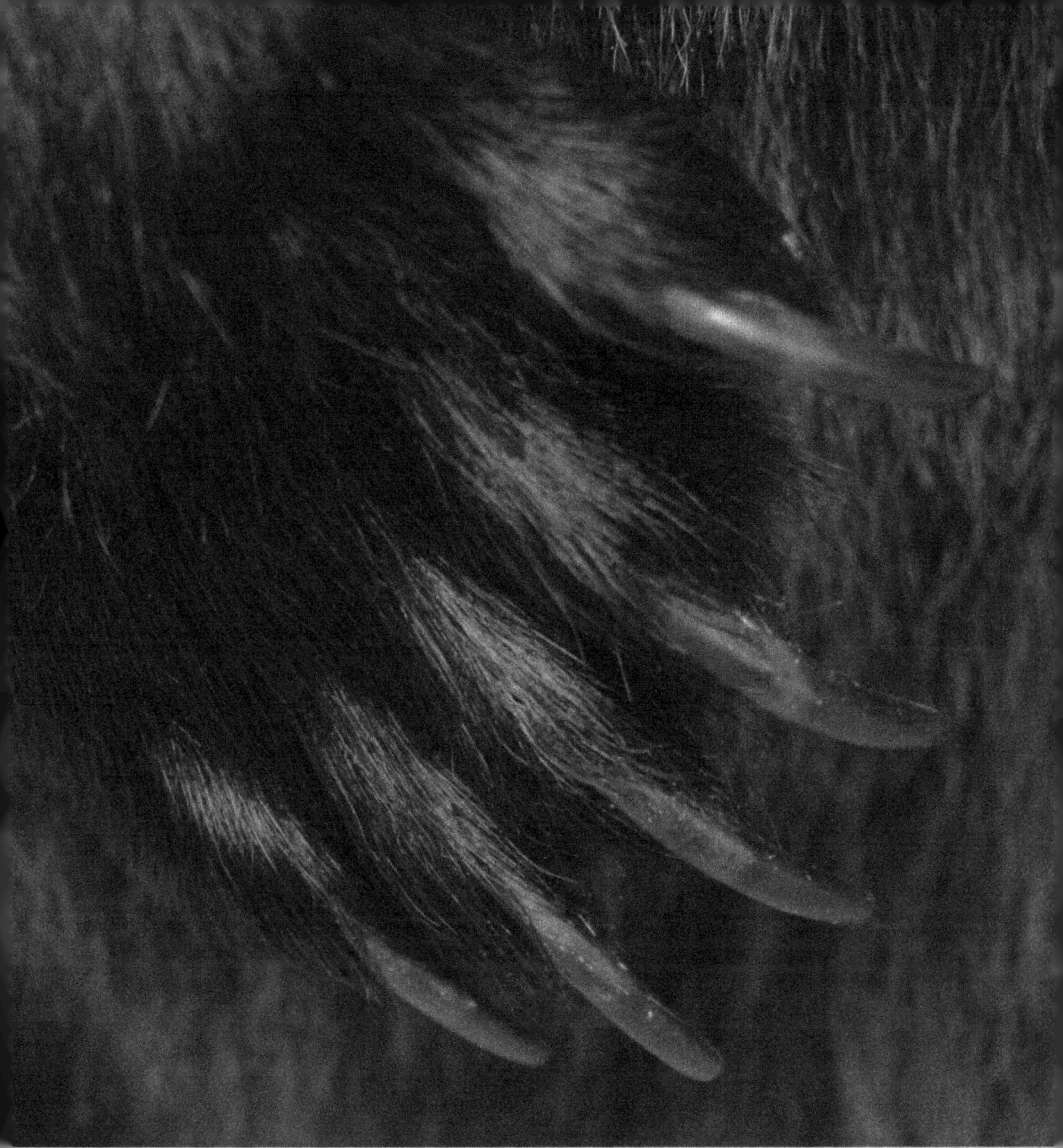

Black bears have short, curved claws. They do not **retract** like a cat's claws. This helps them to climb trees.

Habitat

Black bears are able to **adapt** to living in different habitats. Many are found in forests, mountains, and wetlands.

They prefer areas with lots of trees and plants. The trees provide them with shelter. The plants are a source of food.

Range

Black bears are found in

many parts of North America.

They are found in over forty states in the United States, as well as in Canada and Mexico.

❚❚

Diet

Black bears are **omnivores**.

They eat both meat and plants.

Their diet is made up of salmon,

small mammals, honey, fruits,

and nuts. They may also eat

carrion, or leftovers from

another animal's hunting.

They have a good sense of smell,
which helps them to find their
food.

Hibernating

In the fall, black bears may spend up to twenty hours a day **foraging**. This helps them to get ready for their winter **hibernation**.

They spend the cold winter months hibernating in a den. This is because there is less food available. Sleeping uses less energy than moving around.

Black bears that live in warmer

places where food is available

through the winter may not

hibernate at all.

Communication

Black bears use sound,

scent, and movement for

communication. They have a

special scent that they can

use to mark their **territory**.

Certain movements, like

standing on their **hind** legs or

swiping a paw, can show

aggression.

Mothers and cubs use sounds

like grunts, clicks, and hums to

communicate with each other.

Movement

Black bears can run at speeds of up to 35 miles per hour. This is for short distances. Most of the time, they walk.

Black bears walk differently from some other animals. They walk heel to toe, which is how people walk. Cats and dogs walk more on their toes.

Black bears are very good
swimmers. They have been
seen in lakes and rivers.

Black Bear Cubs

Black bears have a **litter** of up to six babies. Their babies are called cubs. They are blind and mostly hairless when they are first born.

Most cubs stay with their mother for about a year and a half.

The mother protects her cubs

from **predators** and teaches

them how to hunt.

Black Bear Life

Black bears are **solitary**. They spend most of their time alone. When black bears are together, their group is called a sleuth.

Most black bears prefer to have their own **territory**. They may share with another bear if there is enough food.

Black bears climb trees to stay

safe from danger, find food, or

to sleep.

Lifespan

Black bears have been known to live up to thirty years in the wild. Most end up living around ten years.

Black bears that live farther away from humans often live longer. This is because they are in less danger of being hunted.

Black bears in **captivity** may live

longer than wild black bears.

They are safe from hunting and

have enough food.

Population

Black bear populations are currently **stable** in the United States. They are not yet in danger of **extinction**.

Although most populations are stable, some black bears are facing problems like hunting and habitat loss.

The black bears found in Florida

and Louisiana are the most

likely to become endangered.

Living Near People

Many black bear habitats are close to where people live. This can be a problem for bears and people.

Many black bears are killed each year when they are hit by cars as they cross the street.

Bears that are used to eating food from people can become **aggressive**. They may attack people for food.

Helping Black Bears

Although black bears are not yet **endangered**, people want to help them to stay safe.

Groups like the Black Bear Coalition work to **conserve** black bear habitats. They want to make sure black bears have a safe place to live.

In some areas, parks and campsites have added bear-proof dumpsters. This is to make sure that bears won't get too close to humans.

Educating people about the importance of not feeding bears is also helping. Bears that stay away from people are more likely to survive.

Glossary

Adapt: to change

Aggression: using force against another

Aggressive: mean, ready to start fights

Captivity: animals that are kept by humans, not in the wild

Carrion: leftovers from an animal's hunting

Conserve: to protect from loss

Endangered: at risk of becoming extinct

Extinction: when there are no more of an animal left in the wild

Foraging: looking for food

Hind: back

Litter: a group of animals born at the same time

Muzzle: the part of the head in some animals that has the nose, mouth, and jaw

Omnivore: an animal that eats meat and plants

Predator: an animal that hunts other animals for food

Retract: to pull back in

Solitary: living alone

Stable: steady, unchanging

Territory: an area of land that an animal clams as its own

About the Author

Victoria Blakemore is a first grade

teacher in Southwest Florida with a

passion for reading.

You can visit her at

www.elementaryexplorers.com

Also in This Series

Gray Wolves	Sloths	Flamingos	Camels	Koalas	Honey Bees	Pandas
Pangolins	White-Tailed Deer	Orcas	Giraffes	Corn	Meerkats	Echidnas
Walruses	Raccoons	Bald Eagles	Apples	Arctic Foxes	Red Pandas	Cassowaries
Tigers	Ladybugs	Moose	Beluga Whales	Leopards	Elephants	Jellyfish
Binturongs	Lions	Dolphins	Reindeer	Hammerhead Sharks	Hippos	Pumpkins
Peafowl	Chameleons	Florida Panthers	Aye-Ayes	Black Bears	Cheetahs	Manatees
Gingerbread	Polar Bears	Hot Chocolate	Orangutans	Coyotes	Marshmallows	Strawberries

Victoria Blakemore

Also in This Series

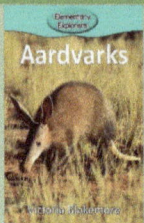

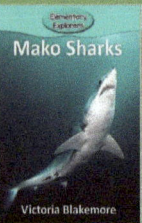

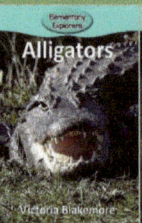

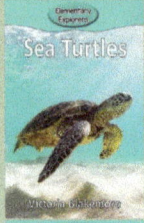

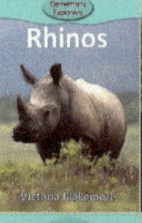

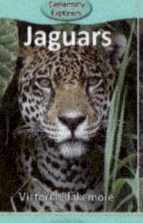

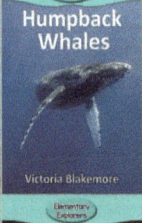

Aardvarks	Mako Sharks	Alligators	Frogs	Hedgehogs	Brown Bears	Bongos
Sea Turtles	Quokkas	Muskrats	Zebras	Red Foxes	Ring-Tailed Lemurs	Platypuses
Anteaters	Kangaroos	Rhinos	Jaguars	Wombats	Capybaras	Gorillas
Cats	Skunks	Butterflies	Dingoes	Snow Leopards	African Wild Dogs	Penguins
Whale Sharks	Wolverines	Warthogs	Caracals	Badgers	Seals	Hummingbirds
Pikas	Humpback Whales	Pumas	Lemonade	Llamas	Tulips	Ostriches
Sunflowers	Fennec Foxes	Sea Lions	Squirrels	Roses	Porcupines	Ice Cream

All titles: Elementary Explorers — Victoria Blakemore

www.ingramcontent.com/pod-product-compliance
Lightning Source LLC
Chambersburg PA
CBHW051250020426

42333CB00025B/3148